BOAT CHILD

A Comedy

other works by Melinda Camber Porter

Non-Fiction
THROUGH PARISIAN EYES

Fiction
THE MALE MADONNA
IMOGEN
FLOATING BOUNDARY
FRANK
BADLANDS

Translation
BARDOT, DENEUVE, FONDA

Plays
NIGHT ANGEL
BOAT CHILD

Poetry and Paintings
THE ART OF LOVE

BOAT CHILD

A Comedy

by

MELINDA CAMBER PORTER

BLAKE PRESS
New York
1993

Front Cover Painting:
Copyright © Melinda Camber Porter
"Parents Waiting"
18"x24" watercolor on paper

Back Cover Author's Photo:
Joyce Baronio

Library of Congress
Cataloging in Publication Data 93-79300

ISBN 0-9637552-0-X

Printed in United States of America

About the Author:

British writer Melinda Camber Porter is a woman of remarkable versatility: a playwright, poet, painter, novelist and journalist. She graduated from Oxford University with a First Class Honours in Modern Languages and then moved to Paris to write for *The Times* on cultural affairs.

Her book on contemporary French culture, *Through Parisian Eyes* (Oxford University Press), was described by the *Boston Globe* as "A particularly readable and brilliantly and uniquely compiled collection," and Joyce Carol Oates wrote, "It is intriguing and very well done."

Her poetry and journalism have appeared in a wide variety of publications internationally, including *The Times*, *The New Statesman*, *The Observer*, *The Times Literary Supplement*, *Le Monde* and *The Partisan Review*.

She is the author of several novels and has just completed *Badlands,* set in the Pine Ridge Reservation in South Dakota.

She worked briefly for the National Portrait Gallery in London and has painted all her life. She is now based in New York, where she lives with her husband and son.

*for my husband, Joe Flicek, and
our son, Robert,
with love.*

BOAT CHILD

A Comedy

in Four Acts

Characters

Characters in order of appearance:

MARILYN, an actress
TONI, the gardener
MALCOLM WAYBRIDGE, a screenwriter
SARA, a guest
GLENDA, a journalist
JOSEPH, a photojournalist
AL SHULMAN, a film producer
PETE, a policeman
MO, the boat child
IMMIGRATION OFFICER

ACT ONE
Scene I

A mansion in Beverly Hills. A ludicrous mixture of Victorian English and Greek styles. A swimming pool is hidden by a row of bright cabanas. The stage is the garden. The house itself is part of the backdrop. One wing forming the dining room is stage right. Hockneys are on the wall. A blazing hot day.

An aged Mexican gardener, TONI, is watering the flower beds.

A fragile, pale, thirty-year-old woman, SARA, drifts into the garden from the house and walks into a cabana. We hear her dive into the pool.

A blonde, very sexy, thirty-year-old woman rushes into the garden and grabs the Mexican gardener.

MARILYN: Life's been so wonderful—since we arrived.

TONI: Thank you.

MARILYN: You know, I don't know how those plants do it. All that mud turned into such lovely, lovely colours.

TONI: Thank you.

MARILYN: No, thank God, Toni.

(MALCOLM, a forty-year-old, British, lean, lanky man rushes towards MARILYN).

MALCOLM: There's a pack of fucking jackals at the door.

MARILYN: I . . .

MALCOLM: I don't want to be manipulated into an interview.

MARILYN: Malcolm—

MALCOLM: Marilyn, you know I hate journalists.

MARILYN: You were a journalist once and I don't think it's right to hide your roots.

MALCOLM: I'm not hiding my roots. And I was only a journalist in order to escape from my roots.

MARILYN: You could have—

MALCOLM: Honestly, Marilyn, you're completely unconscious of politics.

MARILYN: I'm stupid?

MALCOLM: Marilyn.

MARILYN: Mediocre?

MALCOLM: You've got a stupid approach to anything that isn't Beverly Hills.

MARILYN: But you're not Beverly Hills and I love you.

MALCOLM: You love publicity.

MARILYN: They want to interview you, too, honey.

MALCOLM: My ego is already inflated by the Jacusi, toughened by analysis and polished by a cosmopolitan life style and I don't need a journalistic jackal to take a bite out of my carefully nurtured self.

MARILYN: I don't think analysis was very good for you.

MALCOLM: It's made me aware that you have to pay for an honest conversation in LA.

MARILYN: Look here, Malcolm, I had to live with plastic plants in New York and now we've got real sap and real grass under our feet. We've got that great sea and the sun and we've got our bodies back here.

MALCOLM: Do me a favour and get rid of those jour-
             nalists. They've been waiting outside the gate
             for an hour. It's rather bad form especially
             in this heat.

MARILYN: Journalists love waiting. They love the feeling
             they're prying. If I let them in just like that
             they'd think I wasn't worth interviewing.

MALCOLM: I'll call Toni — Toni, can you tell them we're
             on a very long long-distance call.

TONI: Thank you, sir.

MALCOLM: Tell them we're on the telephone.

             (He does sign language.)

TONI: Thank God.

             (He makes the sign of the cross.)

MALCOLM: Yes.

             (Exit TONI.)

MALCOLM: Darling.

MARILYN: Yes, darling.

MALCOLM: I'm delighted you're happy.

MARILYN: Happy? Course I'm happy.

MALCOLM: You like it more than New York or London?

MARILYN: I don't like you in London. You're so English
             in London.

MALCOLM: I'm myself everywhere — but all those hedges
             make me feel I'm back in the suburbs with
             my first wife. I really feel we should move.

MARILYN: We can't. It's like masochism to leave. And
             what about me?

(MARILYN begins to water the plants.)

What about me? It's taken me thirty years to become me and two years to live as me. I'm not giving that up for no one.

MALCOLM: If all the West can produce is ME people and computers—I'd prefer to be—an insect, anything rather than end up looking for ME or the best home computer.

MARILYN: I like being me.

MALCOLM: Masturbation and homosexuality. That's what being me is about. You said we'd have children.

MARILYN: I told you I don't mind adopting. We'll have a nanny and the house is big enough here. Mo sounds perfect. She's past the age of making a mess and howling all night. I just hope that horrible boat trip didn't turn her pathological.

MALCOLM: We're all pathological. It's just a question of different styles of madness.

MARILYN: We've got style.

MALCOLM: Yes. And now I'm delighted to have other people's children, to live in a rented-out film lot, to write about other people's fantasies...after all, living is such a strain, it's healthier breathing from an oxygen tent, and...darling, remind me to replace my solarium lamps...I don't trust the sun.

(SARA appears, dripping wet from the pool.)

MARILYN: Hi sweetie. You like the pool?

SARA: It's absolutely splendid.

MARILYN: You never saw what it was like before we moved in.

SARA: Oh, was it awful?

MARILYN: Naw. Just ordinary.

SARA: Malcolm, I just read this article about a child drowning.

MARILYN: That's why we got the pool.

              (She giggles.)

MALCOLM: Come on, darling. You're late for your gay exercise class. And please don't smash up the car again. *(To SARA.)* She smashes up things when there's no sexual tension.

SARA: Oh Malcolm, honestly.

MALCOLM: Americans do things like that, Sara. You'll get used to it.

MARILYN: He's great. Bye, darling. *(Kissing him.)* You're both so kookie. I can't get that crazy feelin' out o' my head, that kind of feelin' I wanna kill every fuckin' stiff-upper-lipped fucker that used to rule the British Empire. You see I ain't got no class, honey.

SARA: You can't blame Malcolm for his background.

MARILYN: Keep it stiff upper lipped. Malcolm's got a little penchant.

MALCOLM: A what?

MARILYN: They call it a penchant in Paris. A penchant for talking to himself.

              (MARILYN skips off.)

SARA: Malcolm, I'm so...I'm...

MALCOLM: I know, the sky's blue, and the sun's hot. It's beautiful. Splendid.

SARA: I'm so unused to this life, Malcolm. You know what we lived, as children, and I feel so strange here.

MALCOLM: For God's sake, Sara.

SARA: I just feel very strange here. That's all. Malcolm.

              (SARA stands up and stretches.)

              Malcolm, do you realise that we're sitting at the other end of the world? Do you remember when—we must have been three or four—and we'd plan our travels all over the world—the encyclopedias and the maps—no that was later on. I remember how clever you were and how you looked down on me when I—got married—and you were going off to Cambridge and then you threw it all away. You ran away. In fact, you wanted to run away since you were four.

MALCOLM: And now I want to leave again. I can feel the same sense of unreality here. The inner emptiness. The external comfort. I'd leave if it weren't for Marilyn's career.

SARA: I'm sure the Boat Child will help your marriage.

MALCOLM: It's hot, would you like a drink?

SARA: You've been drinking already this morning.

MALCOLM: It's only a facade. I promise you. I appear to be drinking but I'm really drowning my sorrows.

SARA: You can't be sad, Malcolm.

MALCOLM: Yes. I know I can't be sad. I came here to find the real me and discovered that I was just a rather priggish, spoilt, precocious public-school boy. And since I have chosen to be what I am, I will continue to behave as if I never left England.

SARA: Tell me, are you going to give the Boat Child an English education?

MALCOLM: No.

SARA: Are you going to give her a mother?

MALCOLM: She has Marilyn.

SARA: For how long? You've been through two models, three restaurant owners, one pop singer and God knows how many one-night stands in the last five years, and—it was always the same story. I don't think you stayed unmarried for more than one week after the decree absolute.

MALCOLM: I love you, Sara, but I do this kind of soul searching at four o'clock every day with my analyst and then over cocktails with my friends and I can't bear talking about myself anymore. Call it resistance to the truth but if so that's my way of coping with the truth.

SARA: Well I just think it's not—I mean is this a nice place for a child?

MALCOLM: Now don't start comparing Vietnam with plastic homes. People who haven't lived any disaster think they can use those sort of metaphors. Oh yes, says Marilyn, the Boat Child must feel just like we did, when we couldn't get into a hotel late one night in Athens. There is no comparison between living in a fascist country and being involved in a slave-master relationship. Everyone here thinks they can plug into the BBC world service by going to their analyst.

SARA: Malcolm! You're so cold.

MALCOLM: I was always like that. I just thought it politer not to show it. I don't have time for many people. People are business or sex or diversion or a sort of rubbish bin for my affections and with my affections goes a whole gamut of hatred and boredom and bad temper. So you're lucky to be out of the close meaningful relationship we once had—when we were four.

SARA: You've taken on Marilyn's values. But Marilyn's not from your background. I—don't understand how you assimilated all her—dyed hair and her sex and money and publicity obsessions. And our relationship has continued since we were four.

MALCOLM: I like sex and money—and the only problem I have with publicity is that I hate the current mass mythology and I don't wish to be part of a two-dimensional Madame Tussaud's.

SARA: God. It's awful. The way you use the English language.

MALCOLM: On the moon it's doubtful if anyone will speak anything except numbers, buzzes and flashing lights so don't think I'm trying to be futuristic. It's just that I'm being assimilated into LA. Nothing wrong with that, old girl.

SARA: I'm not old. I'm—

MALCOLM: You're as old as your ancestors and as
              anachronistic.

SARA: Well, all I can say is—

MALCOLM: Please don't say anything. I have to admit
              that I need a drink. And you need one too.
              Won't you have one?

SARA: OK. But you're—

MALCOLM: I'm trying to be helpful. It's called consciousness
              raising. Oh God, Sara, you mustn't ask me
              to be a nice person.

SARA: I'm awfully sorry.

MALCOLM: Go into the pool and take a spoonful of sun
              and turn the stereo up—you can hear it
              underwater—Marilyn's brainwave—there's a
              joint in the third drawer down in the cabana—
              and when you're feeling more relaxed we'll
              discuss your divorce and my abysmal
              personality.

SARA: OK, Malcolm, I'll have a try.

MALCOLM: That's it, darling, be a sport.

              (Exit SARAH and enter MARILYN.)

MARILYN: I heard it all. What a—

MALCOLM: Pipe down, darling. I'm listening to myself
              and the birds are listening to each other and—

MARILYN: I'm also reflecting, Malcolm.

MALCOLM: Yes. Poor Sara. She's always been a sacrificial
              victim. Runs in her family.

MARILYN: I decided not to go to the gym.

MALCOLM: I often think that any human being who
              develops a—such a false self must have a lot

of nothingness to hide. Think of all those dark, damp, empty corridors in her mind, all the pipes and dripping water, and the white-washed door that leads into her...emptiness.

MARILYN: It sounds terrible.

MALCOLM: It is, it is. She's cultivated nothing except the right voice and opinions and the right rightness. I hate undressing people like that.

MARILYN: I've been thinking, Malcolm.

MALCOLM: You're right. Sara's so British.

MARILYN: Malcolm. Listen.

MALCOLM: I always listen to you, darling.

MARILYN: I'm getting cold feet. About the Boat Child. It'll be foreign, and won't follow a word we say and it...

MALCOLM: The Chinese have always adapted well in America.

MARILYN: But they're different from us. They got pictures instead of words. They believe in Marx, or Mao, in a person, not in God. I looked it up in the Childrens' Encyclopedia, under CHINA. And it sounded like they're your spacemen talking buzzes and all. I don't want somethin' like the alien in my house. What if it doesn't pick up English quick, and only eats rice and bean sprouts. We'll be eatin' Chinese, or have to drive into town for special takeout Chinese. Another thing I read, they don't like to be people in China. They live in groups. So what if it brings home a whole gang from school every day and has a trauma if we send it to be turned into a ME person, like with analysis, or...

MALCOLM: Yes. You have a point. Our notions of identity won't apply, we'll have to send it to group analysis...Or we could always adopt another Mo. We'll have to think about the trauma, too. People who've been through a war and then that immoral boat trip need to re-adapt slowly. We have to be cruel to be kind. You understand that darling. That's your philosophy with me, isn't it?

MARILYN: We might have a mental patient on our hands. I'm really getting cool about the idea...In fact, I'm really cooling off about the whole deal. If sounds great, but the more I get into the reality, the more it turns me off.

MALCOLM: Of course, we'll have to start off recreating the conditions of its life and then, slowly wean the child from its past. Of course, a child raised in a war situation would be horrified by peace. Its whole metabolism and mental imagery would be geared to coping with horror. So we have to recreate...

MARILYN: Well, we'll be having rows. Isn't that enough?

MALCOLM: No, I think to do this thing properly we have to recreate a sort of austerity here. Her room must be stark with some...straw mats, and we must start growing Vietnamese vegetation in the garden. She must have...intimations of her past—visual stimuli and we must build up our record collection including Vietnamese folk music and lullabies. I've put some hand grenades in the refrigerator.

MARILYN: The fridge.

MALCOLM: They keep better on ice.

MARILYN: In my gorgeous house, grenades? Are you go-
              ing crazy? I just did up her bedroom really
              nice—all bright and lush.

MALCOLM: You have to understand, darling, that we have
              to adapt. That's the role of parents: to adapt
              to a child's needs. And we mustn't impose
              in a colonialist fashion our Western ideas.

MARILYN: Why don't we go and live in Vietnam? Or
              just let the child live in LA? You can't teach
              it to think rubber ducks can fly.

MALCOLM: I'm writing that down. That's a perfect image
              for my screenplay—for that galactic electronic
              rubber duck I've been fretting over. Darling.
              That's such a Walt Disney reference. Lots of
              echoes...mmm...you'll believe a rubber duck
              can fly...what a great sentence.

              (MARILYN sits at his feet and cuddles him.)

MARILYN: I got the part.

MALCOLM: What?

MARILYN: I'll have to dye my hair again.

MALCOLM: But you can't waste all that Actors Studio and
              the Method and my pal from Rada, you can't
              waste all that on a B feature.

MARILYN: But they're spending millions on the publici-
              ty. And I need the money. And I can't keep
              doing roles that *you* think will get me an Oscar.

MALCOLM: Don't I earn enough to give you a real life
              style and to preserve your artistic gifts, and—
              instead of wasting yourself on...

MARILYN: The sort of crap you write. At least I won't
              accept parts as a galactic monster or a Dracula

victim. You wouldn't catch me in one of your vampire, sci-fi screenplays.

MALCOLM: I have to work to earn a living. And you can take the time to learn about being a mother. It's an education for you.

MARILYN: Malcolm. I don't want an education. I want starring roles. I'm going to have a breakdown with all this. Since we arrived life has been a nightmare.

MALCOLM: It is a nightmare. In ten years time Russia will have gained control of Europe. China will have invaded Russia, and the Japanese will have invaded us, so the East will be taking control of the Western World. The Japanese have already beaten us at the economic war. I think we ought to prepare ourselves for the dawning of the Great Red Sun of China, dipping into our Pacific coastline. The sun by that time will be purple from pollution. And the coastline will be covered by a bright yellow protective covering of anti-nuclear tissue to protect us against the effects of nuclear waste washed up on the shore. There'll be no petrol, so LA will be covered by bicycles...that's another thing...a bicycle for the Boat Child.

MARILYN: You've got a real Monty Python sense of humour.

MALCOLM: I'm not joking, darling. Power moves in circles round the world and now it's time for the East.

MARILYN: But, about the house, darling.

MALCOLM: You know, I never realized the Boat Child would prepare us, and teach us inadvertently about coping with the future.

*(SARA appears, dripping wet, from the pool
and stoned.)*

MARILYN: Hi. Honey. You look great.

MALCOLM: Come on old girl. Have a drink.

SARA: *(Dreamily.)* Oh lovely. Super.

MARILYN: We need to find you a guy for the week.
               You can't keep on at Malcolm. He's...

SARA: Underwater I saw your plastic lilies. They're
               beautiful.

MARILYN: I think...Al would be just right.

MALCOLM: Al Schulman? You're joking.

MARILYN: No. He knows everyone and everywhere in
               New York.

MALCOLM: But...

MARILYN: Malcolm.

SARA: We'll go swimming together...in the sea...at
               night...

MARILYN: He's more cultivated than...

MALCOLM: What's the point of him knowing New York
               when...

MARILYN: He can take her...to New York. For a few
               days. On a business...

MALCOLM: But I depend on Al. He's my alter ego—and
               without him, I'd never know what's going on
               in this town.

MARILYN: He loves upper-class women.

SARA: It's so sweet of you to think of...

MALCOLM: You'll have to...

SARA: Oh, don't worry.

MARILYN: Malcolm. Stop telling her what to do.

SARA: Please don't fight.

MALCOLM: Shut up, Sara. We cultivate rows.

SARA: Please...

MARILYN: She's stoned out of her mind...

MALCOLM: Sara has to embrace the New World, a new
               life style, a new attitude to her inner wasteland.
               She has to open up that door and grow some
               new vegetation.

MARILYN: Bean sprouts?...

MALCOLM: Sprout beans? No, she'll sprout sexual fan-
               tasies. The vegetation of erotica, the twisting,
               curling, intertwining Sara.

SARA: It's cold here. I feel awful. I took too much.

MALCOLM: Sara's stoned out of her mind.

MARILYN: I'm not talkin' about Sara.

MALCOLM: Neither am I.

MARILYN: I think Sara should take a walk.

SARA: I'm not a child, Marilyn.

MARILYN: Then, take a walk.

MALCOLM: You don't want an audience, darling?

MARILYN: Listen, Malcolm. I just redid it. Last week,
               the sixth bedroom was repainted spring col-
               ours. Like a bower, a big cradle of—

MALCOLM: It's my house and if I want to make it a home
               for our child I will.

MARILYN: Malcolm, just stop messin' around with other
                people's lives.

MALCOLM: You mean our life?

MARILYN: If you touch our house, I'll kill—you.

MALCOLM: And if you start fucking around the house
                with the Polish, Jewish, Gypsy photographer,
                I'll—

MARILYN: You think I take my clothes off for any crazy
                photographer that comes along? You're the
                one who got me to strip the last time for
                one of your art movies that never got the
                Oscar. Remember, you crazy sonovabitch.

SARA: Malcolm's perfectly sane.

MALCOLM: I am not sane. I am not predictable. And
                if I say I'll do something, I probably won't.
                But, darling, you did meet that photographer
                in Poland. I remember, you met him.

MARILYN: He took me comin' off the plane.

SARA: Who?

MARILYN: Jo Lansky. I think we just gotta let him and
                that journalist in.

MALCOLM: Sara, everything comes and goes. Marilyn will
                tell you how most of her affairs depend on
                what's in or out. She is infinitely adaptable,
                and quite athletic. Go on, darling. Your
                choreographer's waiting. Or is it your Polish
                boyfriend?

MARILYN: I mean it, Malcolm. If you blow up the house,
                I'll leave.

                (Exit MARILYN.)

MALCOLM: And if you don't do what I want you to do, I'll have Sara, won't I darling?

SARA: I never know when you're joking and when you're serious, Malcolm. It frightens me because I do love you, Malcolm, and I've needed to see you for years. I don't understand your way of living and I don't have a life style myself. My children are with their father, but I had to leave them. I wanted to see you, Malcolm.

MALCOLM: *(He stands up and opens a bottle of wine.)* Why me?

SARA: Well, we did love each other as children.

MALCOLM: We still are.

SARA: Which is why we still love each other.

MALCOLM: We do?

SARA: You wouldn't have invited me if you hadn't loved me.

MALCOLM: That's true.

SARA: I wanted to learn how you've changed.

MARILYN: *(Patting her on the head.)* Fantastic, darling. But what about me? I know your world — your dinner parties and class structures and weekends saying the opposite of what you mean. What can you tell me?

SARA: You still say the opposite of what you mean — which is why Marilyn finds you so funny.

MALCOLM: Sara, I know your world which happens to be my world and you have nothing to show me. Nothing new. Only a past I've been try-ing to —

SARA: Deny.

MALCOLM: I admit I'm an overgrown schoolboy.

SARA: I just wonder what you and Marilyn have
                 together.

MALCOLM: Well, she's sexy and I'm clever. And that's
                 why I'm frightened of missing out on a family
                 with her.

SARA: You want a family?

MALCOLM: At least four children in case three of them
                 turn out like me. If I read enough Shakespeare
                 one of them might absorb it in the DNA.

SARA: Why do you always have to be clever? Isn't
                 it enough to—

MALCOLM: We're behaving like children. Just keep look-
                 ing at the blue sky and get your body in con-
                 dition. I'll deal with the journalists and the
                 Boat Child and Marilyn and you. Just take
                 a holiday.

SARA: You hate people who love you.

MALCOLM: You sound like my parents.

SARA: OK, Malcolm. It's a deal.

MALCOLM: A deal?

SARA: I'll have a holiday.

MALCOLM: And if you've come here with the intention
                 of growing up, please do. After a week in
                 this house you'll become as unhappy as we are.

SARA: I'm learning. But I'm not unhappy. It's a
                 wonderful holiday. It's nice to take a holiday
                 from being a mother and a divorcing wife and
                 a rejected wife and a tweeds and pearls lady.

MALCOLM: I can't see you as anything except the little girl whose skirt I looked up one day in the spring in St. James Park when your nanny hit me on the head you giggled. It's—I mean going to bed with you would be like raping a four-year-old child. It'd be like raping my own child. You know, Sara, incest and that sort of thing is the material of Greek tragedy. It's as old as the hills.

SARA: You mean going to bed with me would be old fashioned?

MALCOLM: I'm not interested in going to bed with people I was brought up to go to bed with. That's what's changed. And so I suppose you're not in the running. I'm programmed to be with women like you.

SARA: But Malcolm I wasn't asking you to go to bed with me. I just said—

MALCOLM: I'm thinking about it. Moving Mo's bed. Yours. Mine. My ex-wife's bed. The swimming pool. The shower. The places I choose to make love in. I'm getting the removal people in. I'm beginning to hate Marilyn's objects. Her reindeer clocks, and silver lame bedspreads.

SARA: But Mo might like that.

MALCOLM: I don't.

SARA: Mo's not your child. You don't know her yet. I just wish you'd wait until she arrives before messing up the house.

MALCOLM: It's a pity you don't understand what it takes to take a risk.

ACT TWO
Scene I

The living room is gradually being destroyed. Half-burnt Hockney prints, smashed chandeliers, adorn one part of the living room. The garden is filled with boxes and packing cases. It is raining.

TONI is pulling down some of MARILYN's objets d'art from the bookcases.

SARA dressed in a bright leotard is doing exercises on the floor.

Chinese folk songs drift through the living room.

SARA: Oh Aggression. Oh Pain. Oh Primal Scream. Oh.

TONI: You hurt?

SARA: No. Please, silence.

TONI: Thank God.

SARA: Oh Pain. Ooooooh Aaaaaaah.

(Enter MALCOLM in leotard.)

MALCOLM: Aaaaaaaah.

SARA: Booo booo peeee dooo.

MALCOLM: Silence. It's pain first. Uggggh. Errrrrh.

SARA: Life's just a bowl of...

(Singing.)

I need a joint. I can't get into it.

MALCOLM: Take the—

SARA: OK. I'll give it a try.

(SARA picks up a box and exits.)

MALCOLM: Marilyn...where are you?

                (Enter MARILYN in bathing costume, carry-
                ing a box.)

MARILYN: I'm going back. Back to what it was. I'm get-
                ting the architect in.

MALCOLM: Darling. I want you to tell your story...the
                truth. None of the rags to riches stuff. The
                truth.

MARILYN: I'm not gonna tell the truth—to journalists.

MALCOLM: Oh God. Malcolm. You're getting sick to death
                with Hollywood. Money and lies. Oh God.
                You're getting moral. No, I'm not. You are.
                I'm not. God. I can't even have a normal con-
                versation with myself.

MARILYN: You wanna know somethin', Malcolm?

MALCOLM: Yes. I want to know something. Something
                clear, precise and heartfelt for once.

MARILYN: You're gettin' into a dream. Like in a script.
                Like you're building a set—for the Boat Child.
                And a nightmare crazy set. Malcolm...

MALCOLM: I came here to earn a living—and to give you
                a baby.

MARILYN: A Chinese baby? And what if I don't want
                a baby?

MALCOLM: You said we'd have a family. You promised.

MARILYN: I wouldn't bring a child into a fuckin' replica
                of some Japanese war camp.

MALCOLM: Japanese? How dare you? This is Chinese.

MARILYN: What's the difference? I can't live in this place.

MALCOLM: But a mother has to adapt itself.

MARILYN: It? I'm not it. I'm not a mother. Got it, Malcolm?

MALCOLM: I beg of you.

MARILYN: You're fucking up my house.

                (Enter gardener with rain-drenched journalist, GLENDA, wearing a silver foil raincoat, carrying tape recorder and enormous case. As she takes off her coat, one sees an attractive girl of about thirty, tense, and sinewy.)

GLENDA: Pleased to meet you. God, I feel I'm in London with all this rain. It's taken me thirteen hours to get some LA rain.

MALCOLM: Well.

MARILYN: Hi. Darling. It's great of you to have waited in the car yesterday. Have a drink and a... meal...Chinese? We're into Chinese food.

GLENDA: I'll get my tape recorder on in a sec. But I'd like to get your side of the story first. Just a mother's view. Father can come in later...my, my...are you redecorating?

MARILYN: No. We're getting the place ready...for Mo.

GLENDA: You seem to be moving home...

MALCOLM: Both of use hate LA. We're bored.

MARILYN: Malcolm's ironic. He's English. Everyone hides their hyperactivity in England, don't they? I mean...we're more open and friendly, they say.

GLENDA: So you're—

MALCOLM: I'll talk to you later. Marilyn's the mother,
              as you say, and the real...

MARILYN: Yes. I'm kind of expectant, like as if I'm get-
              ting a nest together...and I feel like...

MALCOLM: Great. Darling, Poo Poo Bee Doo. Bysee Bye.
              Honey. Coo Coo. I wanna...poo.

              (Exit MALCOLM.)

GLENDA: Is he all right?

MARILYN: Malcolm? Oh he's so British. We get along
              like a kind of sea all merging...

GLENDA: And you're going to add another child to the
              family. You already are expecting, you say?

MARILYN: Sure. The Boat Child's here...in the Customs.
              In New York. You know they gotta put them
              in custody before they come into homes...it's
              kinda legal...Malcolm's filled out
              everything...in case they got diseases. I
              remember when I was dancin' roun' America,
              how I got stuck in Customs. Like a parcel.
              They treat you like that.

GLENDA: And why did you decide to adopt a Boat Child?

MARILYN: Malcolm...an' I read a lot of papers...an'
              we decided, havin' looked through the
              papers...to choose people who needed things
              more than we do.

GLENDA: You mean you don't need food and clothing?

MARILYN: We kind of have a good relationship.

GLENDA: But other people need the basics of life more
              than you do?

MARILYN: I kind of like...dancin', an' singing'...an'
              I've been working hard on the special aspect
              of...

GLENDA: Acting?

MARILYN: You see since we arrived Malcolm's been
              workin' like crazy on this science fiction
              idea...it's really horrific...an' contem-
              porary...an' we've been livin' the whole
              thing...together. I've been really involved in
              a more like traditional acting experience. I never
              really got into the Method. An' Malcolm got
              me in a sort of Rada experience.

GLENDA: So the Boat Child's come along at a bad time?

MARILYN: Yeah. Kind of...we're makin' the space
              though...we're redecoratin' the living room
              Chinese style...to —

GLENDA: Do you feel you're the right people to adopt
              a child who isn't used to your life style?

MARILYN: You know, what's your name, honey?

GLENDA: Call me Glenda.

MARILYN: ...You know I find it...like when you're a
              couple...Malcolm's only upstairs. He's a great
              talker...I'm...a...I'm not an intellectual,
              honey. I'll jus' get you a drink an' find
              Malcolm.

              *(Meanwhile, JOSEPH has been standing in the
              rain outside the door, taking photos. He knocks
              softly.)*

GLENDA: Oh. OK. I'll have my drink with Jo...this
              is Jo...Jo Lansky...an' this is...

MARILYN: Feel at home. The drinks are there. The fridge
             is filled with bean sprouts. . .but there's peanuts
             underneath them. . .an'. . .byeee. . .

             (GLENDA gets the drinks.)

JO: She's a beautiful woman.

GLENDA: OK.

JO: Lovely eyes.

GLENDA: I said OK.

JO: Glenda. We came to an agreement.

GLENDA: I'm not a voyeur and I'm bored with our rela-
             tionship, whatever it's called—it was a com-
             promise and it's beginning to feel like one.

JO: You know you're free to join in.

GLENDA: I—want something less—

JO: I know Marilyn. I've met her before. You can't
             call that casual.

GLENDA: I don't care what you call it. I call it sex and
             I'm cutting it out of our rapport. OK?

JO: OK. OK.

             (Sounds of shrieking.)

GLENDA: Oh God.

JO: It sounds like a murder story.

GLENDA: It sounds like copy.

             (Enter SARA. She bumps into GLENDA.)

SARA: Hi.

GLENDA: Hallo.

SARA: Awfully sorry.

GLENDA: Do join us for a drink.

SARA: Oh no. Really, I won't. You wouldn't be interested in me. I'm a childhood friend of Malcolm's. No one creative...or anything special.

GLENDA: Nor are we. Do join us.

JO: You've got lovely legs. Have you ever thought of doing some modelling?

SARA: No.

               (Walks over to a drawer and gets a joint.)

               It relaxes me...and I'm quite nervous with people I don't know.

GLENDA: Do you like LA? I suppose staying with Malcolm must give you insight into the place.

SARA: Well...it's strange...*(inhaling her joint.)* Malcolm...hates my Englishness...and I've travelled a lot with my husband...my ex-husband...on business trips...but I've never tried to participate. I was always a tourist.

GLENDA: And Malcolm's giving you a crash course in his life style?

SARA: I don't know...in the morning there's a pain session...and then I swim, underwater...and Al comes over...there are the plastic lilies...and those huge roses, and fuschia when you come out of the pool, giving off heavy scent...and...the colours go...and when the lights are out...in this room...Malcolm makes me sit here with the papers...reading about Iran...or looking back on old issues on the Horrors of the Boat People.

GLENDA: *(To Jo.)* The girl's upset.

JO: Let her get it out of her system.

SARA: I heard a terrible story in the papers. You know, they—some people adopted a Boat Child, a small baby, and the poor thing drowned in their pool.

GLENDA: I remember. I researched the story.

SARA: I'm here on holiday. It's a nice change.

             (Enter MALCOLM.)

MALCOLM: Hello.

GLENDA: We were just talking about—

MALCOLM: Sara, darling, you've been going a bit heavy on the dope today. I'll get you a raw egg and six pints of water.

             (MALCOLM goes to the fridge.)

             (To the fridge.) Of course you won't be able to tell the real story since the Daily Mail wants some slush about adoption. But I'm delighted you can see that the activity of integrating a traumatized child into a new environment isn't as simple as you might imagine.

GLENDA: Do you—

MALCOLM: I don't answer questions.

GLENDA: Well then there's no point asking them, is there?

MALCOLM: I've been waiting to tell the world something for a long while.

GLENDA: Sara, is she—

MALCOLM: No...

             (Going over to SARA.)
             Well—

SARA: I was just telling them about—that article.

MALCOLM: Sara, darling, Al's waiting to take you scuba diving. In the drive. I won't let him in until the house is properly finished. *(MALCOLM bends down on the floor and listens.)* We've been trying to irrigate...to raise the house on stilts. Oh, and by the way, if you want to help us with the demolition, just go ahead. Don't bother to pick things up...I'm finding my bourgeois habits...be a good boy, Malcolm, stuff...pick up the rubbish, don't drop things, is, thank God, disappearing...it's all—

             (SARA gets up, and staggers to the door.)

             Take an egg with you. And some Perrier. We've told Al to cut out the intoxicants this evening.

SARA: Thanks.

             (MALCOLM paces up and down. Exit SARA.)

JO: I'll leave you to it. *(To GLENDA.)* He's making me nervous. I feel like a bath.

GLENDA: Malcolm. May I ask you a favour?

MALCOLM: I'm not in the mood.

GLENDA: Jo's going to take a bath. Do you have one?

MALCOLM: We have one bath left. For Marilyn. But I'd recommend the hose pipe in the third cabana. There's a beautiful view onto the Pacific from there. Just a personal preference, of course. Do as you please.

JO: Where is Marilyn?

MALCOLM: Swimming. In the rain. In the pool. She's turned up the heating and there seems to be a faulty connection since yesterday. With the rest of the house.

GLENDA: Oh?

MALCOLM: *(Smiling.)* Yes...I...er bombed the garage.

GLENDA: So you're trying to destroy the home—before the child arrives?

MALCOLM: Not quite destroy.

GLENDA: And you don't want your own children?

MALCOLM: Oh I would love to have a small amount of immortality since I'll never get it in my work but Marilyn doesn't like the idea of being bloated for nine months and being limited to playing pregnant mothers in films.

GLENDA: Do you realize that all of this is unquotable?

MALCOLM: No. Why? So?

GLENDA: It's too ironical. If I printed it straight people might get the idea you were a bigoted male chauvinist snob, a kind of disembodied brain without common sense or feeling. Perhaps it might go down well when your friends are stoned or at certain dinner parties, but my readers—For my readers it would be shocking that people would talk so ironically about such a serious subject.

MALCOLM: I—

GLENDA: I just want to get some simple answers to some simple questions.

MALCOLM: If you wants facts, ask Jo. He knows Marilyn probably as well as I do. First meetings are decisive and tell you all you can ever know — about anyone. So tell me about yourself.

ACT TWO
Scene II

*The house is beginning to look like a bomb site. MALCOLM
has evidently begun his reconstruction of a Vietnamese camp.
MARILYN and JO are walking around the debris. He is
taking flash photos of her.*

JO: Just look at this place. It's—like what I saw in Warsaw, when I got back. The man's crazy. Next he'll be starting a movement, getting the rest of California to turn their land into a warscape.

MARILYN: Jo Jo. Cut out the photos. If you print a word about what Malcolm and I's up to, I'll sue you.

JO: Malcolm and YOU? You mean you're in this fuckin' game?

MARILYN: I told him, I can't live here.

JO: Give me a call when you've moved in with the Pope or the Maharishi. It'll be an improvement on this crank.

MARILYN: Malcolm knows politics. It's a political statement. That's what—

JO: I hate to see you like this.

MARILYN: Do I look older?

JO: You look as if you make love to a fuckin' tight-assed fascist. Like you get your kicks out of a mind game. That's what Malcolm is and it's the civilized ones that really know how to go in for the kill.

MARILYN: Malcolm ain't killed no one.

JO: Well. He's blown up your home. There's no bathroom. Fuckin' hand grenades in the fridge.

MARILYN: I—hate it all. I do.

JO: He's blown up your lovely home and stopped
              you from having a child. He's stopped a
              beautiful lady from having her house and kids.
              Just look at yourself and your home. You've
              changed. That man's driven you round the
              bend.

MARILYN: Stop it. I'll cry.

JO: So you're into war? Make war, not love. Fuck
              a mind and that's what you get. It's like ter-
              rorism. Mind terrorism.

MARILYN: You lived the real thing, didn't you? I mean
              you didn't just read it.

JO: Fuck it, Marilyn. I didn't live the real thing.
              I was sent away before the trouble started.
              I don't know the hell what that kind of bar-
              barity feels like. I never lived the war.

MARILYN: You talk as if you know.

JO: I suffered indirectly. And I don't want to know.
              I don't want to get near that shit. Not even
              waste a breath on fuckin' pain. There's enough
              of it—enough.

MARILYN: I know. I hate all this mess. I—keep on
              feelin'—it'll get worse.

JO: It will. That Malcolm game is contagious.

MARILYN: I'm scared.

JO: Glenda's nauseated. But she's just an observer.
              I'm—

MARILYN: You're scared?

JO: I'd just get out quick.

ACT TWO
Scene III

SARA and MALCOLM are sitting on the lawn. It is night.

SARA:	Glenda went off to the Beverly Hills Hotel. She's got another interview. She seemed quite happy.
MALCOLM:	I gave her a whisky. And she told me her life story. It's the only way to deal with journalists. They go around in a mean pent up rage because they're never allowed to talk about themselves. So I interviewed her.
SARA:	Marilyn went off dancing with Jo, after the photographic session.
MALCOLM:	I saw them—making love in the garden. They've met before, you know.
SARA:	Really?
MALCOLM:	Then, you appeared, and they put their arms around you. I expect they wanted a threesome.
SARA:	I didn't feel comfortable.
MALCOLM:	We can talk, if you want.
SARA:	Where's Al?
MALCOLM:	We could fix up Mo's room.
SARA:	I'm quite happy sitting here.
	(MALCOLM puts his hand through her hair.)
MARILYN:	And how are the children?
SARA:	In boarding school.

MALCOLM: And your ex-husband.

SARA: In London. Married to his merchant bank. Liv-
              ing with a—another merchant banker.

MALCOLM: Man or woman?

SARA: I don't know.

MALCOLM: You're prettier than you were.

SARA: In my twenties?

MALCOLM: No. Since you arrived.

SARA: It's the first time—I've had sex.

MALCOLM: Really? With Al?

SARA: I mean, the first time I've let myself go.

MALCOLM: You're in good company. Some of the most
              professional lovers don't get going until their
              middle age. Marilyn's a good example.

SARA: Am I really prettier?

MALCOLM: Yes.

SARA: Marilyn's sexy.

MALCOLM: Well, she's meant to be one of the most
              beautiful women around.

SARA: So you find her—more attractive than me?

MALCOLM: I like your sensitivity. She can look too fleshy.
              Sometimes her sensuality is like a big fur coat.
              It stops one from touching her.

SARA: Sex is very odd around here. It's like breathing.
              It's as if there's nothing else to do.

MALCOLM: Yes. It's rather unpleasant—but Marilyn doesn't
              believe in fidelity.

SARA: You can't bring up a child in this atmosphere.
                 I mean, Marilyn could never look after a child.

MALCOLM: Marilyn's a finished chapter.

SARA: Malcolm, you sound so unconcerned.

MALCOLM: Marilyn and Malcolm lived in a dream world
                 for two years. They loved each other. And
                 Malcolm sat in his garden and waited for
                 another Marilyn. Sara went on holiday to forget
                 her divorce and ended up bang in the middle
                 of another divorce.

SARA: You can't run away.

MALCOLM: From yourself?

SARA: Well, what on earth are we running away from?

MALCOLM: I don't know. Yes. You hid behind a stable
                 marriage. My marriages were never secure.

SARA: Neither was mine.

MALCOLM: We had secure childhoods. Your parents were
                 happy.

SARA: They hated each other.

MALCOLM: So did mine.

SARA: You were spoilt and I was ignored.

MALCOLM: So nothing's changed?

                 (Enter MARILYN and JO.)

MARILYN: Jo Jo. Please. Not yet honey.

JO: Let's all kiss and make up. No hard feelings,
                 Malcolm?

MALCOLM: I'm not in the mood for a punch up. In fact,
                 I'm very overwhelmed, I'm melting under the

rays of your new-found happiness. It is very touching. We were just discussing the romanticism of the evening, Sara and I, the moon, the white hot smell of Marilyn's perfume, her fur-coat sensuality. Can I help you pack?

MARILYN: No. All I want is no hard feelings, like Jo says.

SARA: We could celebrate.

JO: You look beautiful.

MARILYN: Yeah. You look a lot better. Please don't touch me, Jo. Not in front of Malcolm.

JO: I'll take Malcolm off for a little walk. I want to discuss the house, the property. We need to work it out friendly.

MARILYN: Let's kiss. I hate people hurting each other.

MALCOLM: Oh, of course, Joseph. Perhaps Marilyn might fill in Sara with the more unpleasant details of our past life. *(To MARILYN.)* We'll keep our discussions to property, darling.

MARILYN: *(To SARA.)* He's great, isn't he? Each time I left a man they beat you up. But Malcolm's so British.

(Exit JO and MALCOLM.)

MARILYN: Let's take a swim.

SARA: I'm frightened to swim on a drunken stomach.

MARILYN: Here's some coke that'll brighten you up.

SARA: I'll get a joint from the fridge.

MARILYN: But I don't want to swim alone. Be a honey and swim with me.

SARA: OK. Let's have some fun.

MARILYN: Get the fireworks from the fridge. And the whisky. We'll give them a son et lumière, you know like you get in Paris.

SARA: I know. I feel like a joke.

MARILYN: You're really improving, honey.

             (Exit SARA.)

             You're changing so fast.

ACT THREE
Scene I

The living room has been blown up. It is night. Complete darkness.

SARA and MARILYN can be heard in the distance. Lights. MARILYN and SARA are tugging at each other.

SARA: That hurt. Stop it.

MARILYN: Just get yourself a good lawyer, honey. You know you can go to prison for that.

SARA: You threw the thing. You nearly killed me.

MARILYN: You blew up the house.

SARA: I took the grenade out of the fridge. Then, you came along and grabbed the thing. You nearly blew me up.

MARILYN: You bombed my pool, bitch.

SARA: You threw it.

MARILYN: I tried to stop you.

SARA: You threw it.

MARILYN: Sara. I don't care what happened. Whatever happened, you wanted to blow up my house and get my husband. Jus' because you ain't got no sex appeal.

SARA: I wouldn't take anything that's yours. And Malcolm doesn't belong to you. You don't want him.

MARILYN: How do you know? Maybe I want you and Malcolm and Jo. Maybe I want all of you. I want everything. I love Malcolm.

SARA: Really?

MARILYN: I need Malcolm. I'm gonna cry now.

SARA: Poor Marilyn.

MARILYN: When something little goes wrong I get this feeling I wanna kill everyone. I used to be such a gentle little girl. But I always wanted everything.

SARA: So did I. But I just fitted in.

MARILYN: You look like my mother. You look how she would have looked.

SARA: Thanks.

MARILYN: She was the prettiest, silliest woman around. I loved her.

SARA: But you never saw her.

MARILYN: She was like you. I'm sexier than her or you.

SARA: My mother told me we all have a past life. It's to do with our ancestors. We have their blood and all the stories they lived in our veins. And we know in our bones about lives we've never lived. Isn't that a horrid idea. Marilyn?

MARILYN: Shut up. You're scaring me. I hate the past. And ghosts.

SARA: You must have been so unhappy.

MARILYN: Shut up. I'm different now.

SARA: Are you?

MARILYN: I am.

SARA: Plus ça change.

MARILYN: Are you being stuck up?

SARA: I just said the more it seems to change the
             less it changes.

             (They sit in silence for a while.)

MARILYN: Hey, honey. D'you think you'll be happy with
             Malcolm?

SARA: He hasn't asked me to be with him.

MARILYN: You could have a nice family life. Like the
             royals. Two boys who rides horses.

SARA: I've already got a family.

MARILYN: But you're a mother figure. You could have
             millions of them.

SARA: I suppose so.

MARILYN: You like a dull life. So they wouldn't stop
             you from getting excitement. You've got it
             made to be a mother, honey.

SARA: And a wife.

MARILYN: Yeah. A mother and a wife.

SARA: And not a lover. Not really a mistress either.
             Nor a girlfriend.

MARILYN: But you commit yourself. It's really nice. I
             admire it. You'd do everything for Malcolm.
             I wasn't right for him. I'm selfish. I can't love
             no one right.

SARA: But I want to be loved without having to give
             anything.

MARILYN: Like the way people love me?

SARA: Yes.

MARILYN: You ain't got that little girl thing. That's what sends them wild.

SARA: Malcolm's like a bloody mother to you.

MARILYN: Yeah. An' now he can get a little love and protection from you.

SARA: No one ever let me be myself.

MARILYN: No. You'll never get that kind of loving.

SARA: I feel cold. I'm going for a swim.

              (MARILYN swills down some wine. Exit SARA.)

ACT THREE
Scene II

Night. The same bombed-out living room. MARILYN staggers across the stage.

MARILYN: Boo boo. Yipee. My Gad. My Gad. *(She trips over some rubble.)* Gad, there's no lights. Jo Jo.

(JO rushes in from the pool and picks MARILYN up and embraces her.)

JO: My darling. What happened?

MARILYN: I dunno. I got no house.

JO: Poor baby.

MARILYN: Yeah. Look at my nice little nest for Mo Mo.

JO: Oh honey, my darling, are you all right? I'd better get some lights. It's dark.

MARILYN: Don't leave me alone.

JO: I'm just getting some lights.

(Exit JO.)

MARILYN: Oh Gad. I didn't want to do it. You made me hate you.

(Enter JO.)

You know what I'm feeling? I'm feelin' real bad.

JO: You blew up the house?

MARILYN: Jo Jo. I didn't. She did.

JO: Marilyn. You mean Sara? I don't believe it.

MARILYN: You're not scared?

JO: No. What's wrong? I feel I'm smiling at my old friend.

MARILYN: Where? I don't see no one. I thought we were having a romantic affair together. Alone.

JO: It's the place that's familiar. This deathly desolate smell. I remember I used to wander around Warsaw. I thought my parents had to be there.

MARILYN: You gotta be jokin'.

JO: No. It's really deathly here.

MARILYN: Shut up. You're jus' telling me stories to scare me you sonovabitch. So I'll leave Malcolm. I'm frightened. I'm all alone. You're scaring me now.

JO: That's a lie, Marilyn.

MARILYN: Jo Jo. Stay with me. Don't get cross, Jo Jo.

JO: OK, honey.

MARILYN: You're not leaving?

JO: No. You're leaving with me. Remember?

MARILYN: You won't walk out on me?

JO: And what if you throw me out? Come on. You're drunk, Marilyn.

MARILYN: I'm not. I worked it all out. We'll live here. They go back to England. I'll live here with you an' the Boat Child. That'll give Malcolm a holiday. . .Jo. . .it won't work out. It's not gonna work out simple. We're all here. There's too many people, all unhappy, an' this child with no one to be Mummy. You know, I feel sick about her. I do. I can begin to feel her now. Like she's here.

JO: Sit down.

               (She sits down.)

               You like me, don't you?

MARILYN: Sure I do. I hope Mo likes you. You're kinda
               casual. No fuss. No noise. An' you're crazy
               like me. It's great here, isn't it? Like a party
               would be great now. Lights. An' fireworks.
               Let's ring up some friends. Lights an' fireworks.
               I wanna dance.

JO: Dance for me. Not the insurance company.
               Honey, if they heard you they'd think you
               intended to blow up the house.

MARILYN: They'll pay for Malcolm's holiday, the in-
               surance...won't they? And they'll pay for the
               house being done up. How long will it take,
               Jo Jo?

JO: Six months.

MARILYN: Six months? Gad no. I didn't realize. I'd bet-
               ter get on the phone.

JO: We don't have a phone. You blew it up.

MARILYN: We can't have the Boat Child. We haven't
               got the things it needs. No phone. No pool.
               No—Jo—I'll get down—to the police station
               and get it kept in custody. Till we get a phone.

JO: You said a long while ago you didn't want
               Mo. But you can have a child of your own.

MARILYN: I did. I wanted to do somethin' nice for some-
               one. Not like Joan Crawford, killing her
               children. I wanted—

JO: Hush now.

MARILYN: It's eerie here.

JO: Marilyn. You're getting me angry.

MARILYN: You'd hate it. Just imagine it. All that pain for a year, getting full up with water and somethin' kicking you to death inside. An' then what happens if one day you think my God I gotta get away from it for just one day.

JO: It wouldn't be like that. Women are made to change their emotions. It just happens. New hormones. Maternal hormones. You don't have to do a thing.

MARILYN: Jus' like that? No tranquilizers?

JO: Yes. You get it all from your body. I've seen it happen.

MARILYN: It scares the shit out of me. Malcolm says you have to stop being a ME person. An' jus' love a baby. An' then I thought I'm me. That's more than enough, isn't it, Jo? That's more than —

JO: Malcolm gave you his theory. His mind game. You'll see it's nothing to do with anyone else's mind. It's —

MARILYN: An' what am I gonna do with Malcolm?

JO: Being pregnant, it's like being high. Pregnant women are beautiful. Their skin is soft and radiant. They — you'd look beautiful.

MARILYN: Gad, don't go on. I gotta child comin' already. An' all Mo wants is a nice warm bed an' a pretty Mummy all perfumed and gentle to kiss her all night, and a bicycle like Malcolm says an' some kids to roll around with — an' then there's me an' Malcolm fightin' all day an' no home an' no phone an' me all crazy an' drunk, fuckin' around with—

JO: You can't put a child in this madhouse. Not after what she's been through. You know what it's like, feeling unwanted. No home. You can't get your revenge. For what happened to you.

MARILYN: *(Weeping.)* I'll find a real home for Mo. Malcolm's crazy. He'd drive anyone crazy. He's a fuckin' bastard. He's fucked up me and my home—he's—

JO: He's no good for bringing up kids.

MARILYN: No. You keep quiet. I did worse than Malcolm. He just ruined the plumbing. I blew up the pool an' the phone.

JO: You'd be a great mother.

MARILYN: I blew up my baby's home.

JO: You blew up Malcolm's home.

MARILYN: I gotta get that child. I gotta make a change.

(Enter PETE a Policeman.)

PETE: Hello, Marilyn.

MARILYN: Gad. It's spookie. I was just about to ring you. I thought it might have been the freezer that blew up. I just heard this bang. Have a drink, Pete.

PETE: I've had Immigration on the phone. Mo Hu Chin is arriving tonight in New York and they couldn't get through because the phone's been blown up.

MARILYN: Gad. My agent. I bet he's been trying to get through. And poor Mo. She'll have nowhere to stay. We'll take her away from all this shit.

PETE: Can I take a statement from you?

MARILYN: Gad. No. I'm shell shocked. Are you crazy? You need a drink.

PETE: I heard you were trying to make alterations to the house.

JO: Alterations? Poor Marilyn. She was trying to get a drink and the freezer blew up.

PETE: Can I take a look?

MARILYN: There ain't no freezer. It blew up. In pieces. Sara did it, by mistake getting me whisky.

JO: I suggest you leave Marilyn in peace. She's had a bad shock. I'll get Malcolm down to the station tomorrow.

PETE: Is he around?

JO: He's at a conference on Primal Disorder Therapy.

PETE: PDT. Oh, I know it. It really helped my wife.

JO: The only problem is Malcolm.

PETE: What do you mean?

MARILYN: He means Malcolm's a problem. He means go gentle. Malcolm hates being questioned.

PETE: I've dealt with artists.

JO: No. He's different. He's crazy. Psychotic. I mean really crazy.

PETE: Violent?

JO: We're worried about him and the child. You know he's started going mad since this Boat Child thing.

MARILYN: Yeah. I don't trust a psychotic with a child. Would you?

PETE: So, you're divorcing?

MARILYN: Yeah. I'm getting a plane to New York to pick up Mo an' take her way from this madhouse. This place ain't right for a child.

PETE: So, you're splitting from Malcolm?

MARILYN: Yeah. That's it. We are. Get me a drink, Jo Jo. Yeah. We're over. Malcolm's gone round the bend.

PETE: I'll ring Immigration.

MARILYN: Do that. I'll be down to the station.

                (Exit PETE. Enter JO from right and SARA and AL SCHULMAN from left. SARA appears to be in a trance. AL is rather drunk.)

MARILYN: My Gad. She's disappearin'. I gotta get her, Jo. She'll fall in the pool, it'll be too late — she'll kill herself. Jo Jo. Stop her. It's my fault. I was cruel.

                (Running after SARA.)

JO: Marilyn. Please —

MARILYN: I'm stoppin' her, Jo. It's dark. She'll go sad. She'll be thinkin' there's no one to pull me out and the pool is warm and the air freezin'.

JO: *(Holding back MARILYN.)* Don't be crazy.

MARILYN: Everythin's eatin' me up. Like everythin' I do
              eats me up. We're all goin' that way. Dark
              and wrinkled. We can't beat it now. It's always
              there. Each night. Comin' to remind us, all
              black in our eyes.

JO: Hold me, honey. What's that you're starin' at?

MARILYN: Sayin' hallo. Hidee, Norma.

JO: Who's Norma?

MARILYN: Hidee, honey. Comin' home with me tonight?
              You gotta nerve sayin' no. No one says no
              when I got an eye on them.

JO: She's gone. Sara's gone. It's OK.

MARILYN: Mama. Mama. Don't leave me.

JO: It was Sara, darling.

MARILYN: Mama. Don't leave me.

JO: Come on, honey. You need a hot bath. Take
              a good long cry. We're goin' to say goodbye
              to the night. We'll go down to a club. A
              nice meal. Soft lights. An' then we'll get on
              a plane an' get your baby. Come on, babe,
              you can't go on hurtin' yourself. It'll be dif-
              ferent tomorrow.

(Exit MARILYN and JO.)

ACT FOUR
Scene I

Next morning. GLENDA and TONI are tidying in the living room and garden.

GLENDA: You take the broom.

TONI: Mrs. Please, no. Five o'clock.

GLENDA: Toni. You've got a baby. What's his name?

TONI: Bard.

GLENDA: Would you like him to come home to this?

(GLENDA takes the hose and waters down the surface of the living room.)

TONI: I sleep.

GLENDA: Yes, I'm asleep. But we've got to disinfect the place before Mo arrives.

TONI: Take a priest and burn it. Exercise.

GLENDA: You mean exorcize?

TONI: Noee. Take a joke.

GLENDA: Mmm. The dawn's so wonderful here. And the sun. You know in England the weather is unpredictable. It's wonderful for a young child here. But after the age of eight I'd give my child an English education. What are the schools like here?

TONI: My son in film school. *(TONI pats GLENDA on the back.)* You marry Mister Malcolm?

GLENDA: No. I've got another job in San Francisco. I don't think he'd keep up with me.

(TONI starts scrubbing down the floor. The sun comes up. AL SCHULMAN stumbles across the living room and stares at GLENDA.)

AL: Seen Sara?

GLENDA: Give me a hand, Al. Take the other broom. No...Like that. *(AL dances with the broom.)* A child's arriving. Would you like your son to arrive home to this?

AL: I'll call my maid. You can have her for the day.

GLENDA: No. I want to help you. It's a new form of therapy. Broom therapy. It's really catching on. Everyone's doing it.

AL: Great. What d'you think of when you're doin' it?

GLENDA: You think about a dirty floor. And then you imagine what it would be like clean. And you aim to get the image in your head realized on the floor.

AL: Hey, say it again.

GLENDA: It's tough, Al.

(MALCOLM appears in towelling robe.)

MALCOLM: Al. My God. Where is everyone at?

AL: Take a broom, Malcolm.

MALCOLM: Glenda—

GLENDA: I got an electrician from the Beverly Hills Hotel.

MALCOLM: What about Jo and Marilyn?

GLENDA: We didn't have anything, Jo and I. It's not too much of a disappointment. It was an arrangement, Malcolm. Take a broom.

MALCOLM: You shared the same room.

GLENDA: It could have worked out. But that's life, isn't it, Malcolm? You lose an arrangement, and something else comes along. I'm off to San Francisco tomorrow to do a piece on life styles. So one never knows.

MALCOLM: This acceleration of life...Marilyn. You...Who's...relating to whom. How many days...how many seconds. Milliseconds. How many lives can you get into one life, Glenda? How many cities can you fit into a day? How many days does a city deserve? Or you or me? Or Marilyn? How much time...being a journalist must help...

             (SARA staggers in. MALCOLM rushes over to her.)

GLENDA: My God.

SARA: Black.

             (MALCOLM carries her to the centre of the stage and lays her on the floor.)

GLENDA: She's bleeding. But not profusely.

AL: God.

MALCOLM: She's slashed her wrists.

AL: My third wife did it. You gotta stop the flow. Here—like this.

GLENDA: She's passing out.

MALCOLM: She's freezing.

             (TONI falls to his knees and prays.)

GLENDA: Can you hear me?

SARA: Take me away.

GLENDA: We're all here. Hold on. You're safe with us.
                Rub her feet.

SARA: Malcolm. I want you.

GLENDA: Hold her, Malcolm, you cunt.

SARA: Malcolm. You're crying. Is it you? Hold me.
                Quick. Hold me, Malcolm.

MALCOLM: You're crying, Sara. Not me.

GLENDA: Hold on. You're OK.

SARA: Glenda?

GLENDA: Yes. It's me. I'm here. Malcolm's here. You're
                right and snug.

                (SARA sobs.)

AL: *(To GLENDA.)* I never knew about this.

GLENDA: Al, she's just a child.

AL: I had a feeling last week she was with me.

GLENDA: Shut up, Al. This has nothing to do with
                you or me or sex.

AL: I don't like it, Glenda. My fourth wife went
                off with the gardener.

GLENDA: Shut up, Al.

SARA: It's warm.

AL: Look here, Malcolm, I like Sara a lot. I don't
                want no swappin'.

GLENDA: Will you ring your analyst?

MALCOLM: Her pulse is regular. There's some brandy in
              the third drawer of the cabana. Can your chauf-
              feur pick up some curtains?

AL: Who's fuckin' who, Malcolm?

GLENDA: We're not fucking anyone, OK? Let's take a
              walk and discuss our predicament. OK, Al?

AL: Where to?

GLENDA: A swim?

AL: You British women. Each one' crazier than
              the next. I'm coming. This is great.

              *(AL puts his arm round GLENDA and they
              exit to the pool.)*

MALCOLM: They've gone. To discuss why neither of them
              are fucking you or Jo.

SARA: You've got to understand.

MALCOLM: I don't have to understand, Sara. I don't want
              to understand.

SARA: She hates children. She didn't want Mo. All
              she wanted was her Hockney an' her couch.
              And that gold statue of herself. In the hall.
              I threw it in the pool. I blew up her phone
              and her pool. And—

MALCOLM: And me?

SARA: I loved you, Malcolm.

MALCOLM: I told you you had nothing to offer. I said
              I didn't like you. But, you know, Sara. I do.

SARA: I'm not sexy. You need a sexy woman.

MALCOLM: I don't know what the word means.

SARA: You'd get bored.

MALCOLM: Shall I spell it out?

SARA: Yes.

MALCOLM: I want to give it a try.

SARA: Fuck you.

MALCOLM: What do you want me to say?

SARA: If you don't know, don't say it.

MALCOLM: I've said it.

SARA: You know something, Malcolm?

MALCOLM: I don't know anything. Is that what you're telling me I know?

SARA: Your sentences are obtuse.

MALCOLM: What I mean by sexy? Is that the question?

SARA: We slash our wrists on the way to the airport. It's just a slashing. And a fucking. And is that how you want me to feel?

MALCOLM: I don't know. I suppose we could be about four or five, couldn't we? You can go back like that, can't you? Great men have been known to have a repeated adolescence.

SARA: You said fucking me would be programmed.

MALCOLM: I feel as if I'm about five. And you're four.

SARA: You said I had nothing to teach you.

MALCOLM: You were sitting in your little dress and I fancied you. That's a childhood romance. It's a nice idea, Sara.

SARA: It's not what you said.

MALCOLM: Is what I say anything to do with what I am?

SARA: Saying and doing.

MALCOLM: This world is changing so fast no one can say what they feel since feeling is related to the environment and we're being sparked off nonstop by so many current ideologies, you know.

SARA: Did Marilyn ever say she was bored?

MALCOLM: No.

SARA: I am.

MALCOLM: I said I wanted to try.

SARA: I didn't.

MALCOLM: No?

SARA: Yes.

MALCOLM: No.

SARA: Yes.

MALCOLM: No.

SARA: Why not?

MALCOLM: Why not?

SARA: I had a family, and children. You had Marilyn and LA. I can't see anything that could make us happy together. Your lifestyle is a joke. My lifestyle is a convention. I hate you, Malcolm.

               (Enter GLENDA.)

GLENDA: Are you two finished? Can we clean up the place, now that—

MALCOLM: Thanks, Glenda. I do appreciate—

GLENDA: Let's stop messing around. Mo's arriving and I haven't got the faintest idea who will parent her. Al, Marilyn, you, Sara—I'm aware that this child will be walking straight into a bloody madhouse. And I feel that as adults we have a responsibility to do something about it—within our very obvious limitations.

               (Enter AL.)

AL: Er, Malcolm, I got really bad news.

MALCOLM: *(To SARA.)* That means no news.

GLENDA: What is it, Al? *(To MALCOLM.)* Will you keep quiet, Mr. Waybridge?

AL: The, er, child—Immigration won't let you have it. They were informed you were, er, mad.

MALCOLM: I don't understand.

AL: Marilyn—

GLENDA: It's perfectly true—

AL: Marilyn told them you'd blown up the house and she took custody. Don't get sore, Malcolm. It happened to me with my first wife. She was an alcoholic. But the judge ruled—you know the diapers, Malcolm.

MALCOLM: I don't believe it.

SARA: She never wanted a family.

GLENDA: She didn't want—Malcolm's family. That's all. It's simple.

MALCOLM: Um. I don't believe she's changed overnight. What happened, Sara?

SARA: All I said—was plus ça change.

MALCOLM: The more it changes, the less it changes?

SARA: That's what I said.

MALCOLM: I think she wanted to be like you. The mother
              bit.

SARA: Really?

MALCOLM: I think we all wanted to change. I think—I
              don't think I'd be good for anyone. I think
              I'm—

SARA: Stop thinking, Malcolm, for once. What do
              you want?

MALCOLM: I'm—I don't care about what I want. I've always
              got what I wanted. The question is—Sara—
              what do you want?

SARA: I'm like everyone else. Malcolm. Dear.

MALCOLM: You're not.

SARA: I'm not special.

MALCOLM: Why not?

SARA: I'm unremarkable.

MALCOLM: Why not?

SARA: I'm ordinary, Malcolm. Don't try and build
              me up.

MALCOLM: Please stop it.

SARA: I'm like anyone else.

MELCOLM: Don't.

SARA: I'm unremarkable.

MALCOLM: You can't disappoint me.

SARA: I can.

MALCOLM: I found something in you.

SARA: You'd find it in anyone.

MALCOLM: Sara. I'll cry if you go on.

SARA: Marilyn's special. I'm not. I'm ordinary.

MALCOLM: I was programmed to like women like you.
             I went to parties with women like you. You
             came here, you tried to change. You have.

SARA: And the Boat Child? And Marilyn? And Jo?
             They're special. They've been through
             something. You haven't. I haven't. We're
             nothing.

MALCOLM: Protected?

SARA: Politics, Cambodia, boat children, Japan, the
             dollar. You're like the newspapers and my last
             husband. It's all so important as long as you
             read it in the papers. Or—you can talk,
             Malcolm. This whole trip of yours was a joke.
             You're—the same. And I am. We're watching
             life and who on earth would want that other
             kind of life, Malcolm?

MALCOLM: Which life?

SARA: Marilyn, Jo, Mo, Glenda. We live outside all
             that.

MALCOLM: Which life?

SARA: The unsafe life.

MALCOLM: You're special.

SARA: Thanks.

MALCOLM: I'm sorry.

SARA: OK.

MALCOLM: You're making me cry, Sara.

SARA: Shall I read it in the newspapers? The way
               you cried when Marilyn left with the child
               you wanted, and your childhood friend slashed
               her wrists after a week in your house?

MALCOLM: So you're leaving me, like the rest of them?

SARA: I'm not leaving. I'm just criticizing you.

               *(They embrace. And as they fall to the floor,
               the Boat Child, MO, appears with the IM-
               MIGRATION OFFICER.)*

OFFICER: Er, Mr. Waybridge. Your, er, wife changed
               her mind. She wants you to keep the child.

               *(MALCOLM and SARA walk towards the Boat
               Child.)*

CURTAIN

THROUGH PARISIAN EYES:
Reflections on Contemporary French Arts and Culture

by
Melinda Camber Porter

Previously published by Oxford University Press

Melinda Camber Porter has interviewed the most prominent Parisian cultural figures of the '70s and '80s. The dominant trends in French artistic and political thought emerge vividly from this array of portraits and dialogues. As a whole, *Through Parisian Eyes* creates a seamless and revealing portrait of French culture.

"For those passionate about French arts and culture, Melinda Camber Porter's *Through Parisian Eyes* is like a daylong trip to the candy store. Porter's eclectic gathering provides an area of interest for almost every palate. A well-rounded, intelligent look at the contemporary Parisian spirit."
San Francisco Chronicle

"A particularly readable and brilliantly compiled collection. The voices of French intellectuals mingle in this uniquely constructed volume of interviews and commentary."
The Boston Sunday Globe

"An inviting opportunity to tap into Paris' thinking...thanks to Porter's willingness to listen well and challenge when necessary."
The Philadelphia Inquirer

"The issues that are raised in *Through Parisian Eyes* are intriguing. It is very well done."
Joyce Carol Oates

"Through Melinda Camber Porter's probing interviews the rich, varied cultural world of Paris springs to life. No cultural critic has produced more revealing, more witty portraits of leading French writers, artists, and political figures. In *Through Parisian Eyes* they reveal themselves in their brilliance as well as in their occasional outrageousness." **Thomas Bishop** (Chairman, Center for French Civilization and Culture, New York University.)

Da Capo Press, New York
priced at $13.95
paperback ISBN 0-306-80540-5
Da Capo Press, Inc.
233 Spring Street
New York, New York 10013-1578
PHONE ORDERS:(800) 321-0050 FAX ORDERS: 212-463-0742

BADLANDS
a novel by

Melinda Camber Porter

Praise for **BADLANDS**

"**BADLANDS** is an extraordinary book. Its imagery makes one think of William Blake. Better than a novel, it reads like a fierce poem, with a devastating effect on our self-esteem." **—LOUIS MALLE**

"**BADLANDS** is lyrical, but unflinching on Native American issues." **—PETER MATTHIESSEN**

"**BADLANDS** is a very strong, very intelligent and very intriguing novel." **—JOYCE CAROL OATES**

"**BADLANDS** is a lovely book, with this strange plangent cry through it. Part journey going forward and backward at the same time. The voice of the narrator strikes an odd chord-mix of selfishness and self hatred, but the tragedy of the death in it is, it seems to me, something that escapes mere symbolism because the weight of the writing is so good. The book is beautiful. It is a prose poem but is absolutely specific about the American landscape." **—MICHAEL HASTINGS (British playwright)**

BADLANDS is set in the forgotten soul of America, the open expanses of the Pine Ridge Reservation in South Dakota.

The narrator, a young Englishwoman, discovers her own history of abuse through the lives of the Sioux. She forms a passionate bond with an adolescent Sioux girl, Minnehaha, and her charismatic father, Blackfoot. A kind of love emerges between them that transcends politics and destiny.

BADLANDS unmasks the march to genocide of Native Americans, and bids us to remember and transcend.

FRANK
a novel by

Melinda Camber Porter

SAUL BELLOW's praise for **FRANK**:

> "The great 'meltdown' of modern sexual anarchy is the real subject of Melinda Camber Porter's novel **FRANK**. To judge by the electronic speed of her narrative and the Stendhalian decisiveness of her characters she has learned all there is to learn about the anarchic phase (if it is a phase). Nevertheless she has some hope for a post-anarchic future. Even now, she seems to say, love is possible. A *kind* of love, perhaps. *Some* kind of love. Readers will understand, without coaching, what she means."

FRANK is set in the lavish backdrops of the international jet set, the hotel bedrooms, beaches and loneliness of Los Angeles, Geneva, London and Paris. This world of materialism has long been experienced, by our heroine and narrator, as a place with no succor and no meaning.

FRANK's heroine (the heir to her sculptor grandfather's priceless oeuvre) is looking for a way out of the empty relationships and the transience. Sex is her currency and language, and her chosen way of breaking out of the circle of loneliness.

On one of her innumerable flights, she picks up Frank, a fellow wanderer, a wheeler dealer whose career as a rock singer ended abruptly and mysteriously. He is obsessed about his former wife, Marina, who now lives with a messianic figure, a sort of retired Jim Bakker, in their mansion in Geneva. Frank lets it be known that he is filled with guilt because he suspects his wife accidently killed their child during one of her orgiastic violent parties. Our narrator heroine, who is now fully in love with Frank, decides to investigate and bring back her own truth.

NIGHT ANGEL
A Musical

Lyrics and Book by
Melinda Camber Porter
and Music by
Carman Moore

NIGHT ANGEL is a poignant and witty, one-woman musical, about a woman's efforts to make a new life in the aftermath of her divorce from a wealthy, domineering man. The woman, Amy, our heroine, is a cabaret singer. She is passionate, insecure and so used to dependency that she can't get back on her feet and work.

NIGHT ANGEL takes us from the lonely distraught woman, afraid to step out of her apartment, to the glorious musical and personal rebirth of our heroine. It is set in the Newark Airport bar where she sings and used to sing before she was catapulted into a life of wealth.

NIGHT ANGEL'S dramatic progression shows how Amy emancipates herself from her 'mating ritual' in the lounge where she would use her singing as 'mating call' to pick up men. This was how she met her first wealthy husband. But, this time round, we witness how she puts an end to her self-destructive game. We see her become herself.

NIGHT ANGEL tells this story through 17 songs and the video backdrop (which is the "book") of the musical. This is a one-woman show with only our heroine and a rock band on stage and with the audience in the bar as the actual theater audience. **NIGHT ANGEL** presents song styles ranging from hard rock to mystic ballad to waltz, all strong on melody, rhythm and unexpected harmonies.

About the composer Carman Moore
Carman Moore, New York-based composer and conductor has one of the most varied careers in American music. Among his commissioned orchestral works have been WILDFIRES AND FIELD SONGS for the New York Philharmonic, Pierre Boulez conducting. He served for several years as music critic and columnist for the *Village Voice*. Highly respected as a composer for dance and theater, amongst his scores for dance are GODDESS OF THE WATERS, choreographed by Alvin Ailey for the Ballet Company of La Scala, and works for Donald Byrd and Ruby Shang with whom he has individually won Meet the Composer Award (1988) and Composer/Choreographer Award (1992).

His musical WILD GARDENS OF THE LOUP GAROU (to poetry by Ishmael Reed and Colleen McElroy) was commissioned by the Music Theatre Group and produced at New York's Jusdon Memorial Church and at the Bayview Opera House in San Francisco. His 1989 Musical PARADISE LOST (with text by Oyamo) was produced at New Dramatists.

FLOATING BOUNDARY
a novel by

Melinda Camber Porter

FLOATING BOUNDARY is a novel of epic proportions set in Hong Kong in the decade preceding 1997, the year China will take control of the colony.

Into the life of British expatriate Geoffrey Lipton, the chairman of a vast conglomerate, steps Anna, a photographer on vacation in Hong Kong. During a day trip on Geoffrey's yacht off Saikung, they sight a woman drowning, while trying to swim the five-mile stretch that separates Hong Kong and China. They rescue her, and later discover her reasons for escape.

Han is the daughter of a disgraced politician and is married to one of the leaders of China's Democracy Movement. Feeling her husband chose politics instead of her (when he knowingly committed acts that would lead to his imprisonment), she half tried to swim, half tried to drown herself, in desperation. Love, not politics, was her motive for escape.

Han and Anna develop a firm friendship. Unknowingly they become twin obsessions for Geoffrey, who cannot decide between them. Into this emotional web steps Jerry, an American who works for the UN High Commission for Refugees. An American presence in a world dominated by tradition brings new solutions and new conflicts.

FLOATING BOUNDARY shows us the real boundary between freedom and tyranny, in the heart and in a nation's identity.

IMOGEN
a novel by

Melinda Camber Porter

IMOGEN is set in the bucolic lakeside estate in Geneva where film director, Clive, and his wife Imogen make their home. Clive has just suffered a nervous collapse which obliged him to leave the set of his movie, *Twilight Games*. Clive believes his dissatisfaction with his career prompted his collapse: for years he has been making films with the sole aim to make money, despite his brilliant early artistic success.

Thus, back at home, he searches for a project that will give meaning to his life. The religious Catholic nanny who cares for his son, Alex, becomes his new subject and eventually his mistress. Juliet's faith in Christ is metamorphosed into a boundless passion for Clive.

As Juliet is plunged into passion and a brusque sexual awakening, she tries, against all odds, to awaken mutual feeling and empathy in a man whose character is marred by indifference and a cold heart.

IMOGEN is a moving novel about a girl's passage from fervent innocence to experience and a man's quest to return in time to the innocence and the authenticity of his youth.

THE MALE MADONNA
a novel by

Melinda Camber Porter

THE MALE MADONNA is a poetic, harrowing tale of a young woman's first passion. Set in Paris and Antibes, in the milieu of the Parisian intelligentsia, the narrator and heroine, Lou, tries to find her identity through an adulterous affair.

She begins keeping a diary of her passion and soon the reality of her daily life, her job and her marriage becomes subordinate to her journal. Within weeks, her hold on reality is lost and her "real" life has become immaterial to her as the diary she keeps becomes her true reality.

She tries to turn her journal into a novel, provoking dramas and twists of fate so she can feed her story. Then, in a final act of submission, she gives up her narrative voice to her lover and he, a journalist, too, takes on the task of completing the novel. In this world of shifting realities, only the written word prevails.

THE MALE MADONNA is a powerful reflection on the nature of reality and the supremacy of the imagination.

THE ART OF LOVE
Love Poems and Paintings

by
Melinda Camber Porter

"Not since William Blake has an artist created such a profound relationship between the visual and verbal worlds. Melinda Camber Porter's vision is subtle, lyrical and has universal significance." **—LEO CASTELLI**

"Melinda Camber Porter's poetry and paintings have a soft, lyrical quality which is intensely attractive."

—ISHMAEL REED

"The great meltdown of modern sexual anarchy is the real subject of Melinda Camber Porter's work. Nevertheless she has some hope for a post-anarchic future. Even now, she seems to say, love is possible. A *kind* of love, perhaps. *Some* kind of love. Readers will understand, without coaching, what she means." **—SAUL BELLOW**

Inspired by William Blake's *Songs of Innocence and Experience*, Melinda Camber Porter sets out to explore desire and give it a pictorial and lyrical form. She takes us on a journey from the loneliness of unrequited love through the ecstasy of sexual pleasure into glimpses of the infinite and transcendent experience of love. Her vision is intensely personal and autobiographical, the paintings telling a decipherable story that springs from her poetic vision.

Writers and Readers Publishing, Inc.
P.O. Box 461 Village Station
New York, New York 10014

Formats: thirteen color plates in
trade paperback original $14 ISBN: 0-863-16-167-7
hardcover edition $28 ISBN: 0-863-16-168-5

Distributed to the trade by:
Publishers Group West 1-(800) 365-3453
Individual Orders through:
Writers and Readers: Tel 212-982-3158, Fax 212-777-4924